YOU ARE FREE
TO WORRY NO MORE

WILLIAM V. MCDONALD

New Life Ministries, Inc.
Austin, Texas
and
HaKesher, Inc.
Tulsa, Oklahoma

Published by New Life Ministries, Inc.
7809 Callbram Lane
Austin, Texas 78736
and
HaKesher, Inc.
9939 S. 71st East Avenue
Tulsa, OK 74133-5338
www.hakesher.org

First Printing June 1999

Cover design by Kenny Mullican and Chad Cox
of Catalyst Productions www.catalystweb.com

Printed by Western Printing Company, Inc.
in the United States of America

Typeset in Garamond
by Kenneth R. Mullican, Jr.

Library of Congress Catalog Card Number
99-95218

ISBN 1-891341-06-5

This essay is dedicated to
my family, whose love is the strength of my life
and to all of our wonderful friends who have enriched
our lives through their friendship in the Lord.
Love to each of you.

מליבי באהבה

TABLE OF CONTENTS

PREFACE

Many years have come and gone since I embarked upon this journey of walking free from worry. Still I thank the Lord because He taught me how to use His word, His principles, and wash away the effects of worry from my life. I think back over twenty years when I was first starting my journey in living a godly life. I had just lost my younger brother. The year was 1978, and I knew very little about the nature of God.

One morning I heard a voice inside me saying, "Go to the county jail and share what Jesus has done in your life." At that time I did not want to obey those words and my emotions were telling me all the reasons why I could not and should not obey. I wanted to know God and I wanted to do what was right. A few days later a man walked into my business who was the director of a local ministry. It was a county and state jail ministry called Faith, Hope, and Love. I remember telling him about how I felt that God was speaking to me, directing me to go to the jail and share what He was doing in my life.

To my surprise that Friday night I found myself standing in the outer room waiting to enter the county jail. I did not know anything about teaching or preaching. I only knew that God had told me to go, and I did. I gave myself to God in that work for over three years, and during that time, I became known among those in the jail. "Preacher," they called me, and all I was doing was sharing my simple testimony. During the latter part of the third year I met a young boy who asked me questions that went beyond my simple testimony. By that time I allowed myself to think of myself more highly than I should; i.e., I gave him answers which I did not truly know to be the correct answers.

After I came to know this young man, I learned that he was serving a life sentence. I began to think about how this young man would try to live his life from what I had shared with him. How he would place his trust in me and believe what I had shared with him about God was true. I cried out to the Lord asking Him to help me, to teach me how to know His words. Thus, my journey had begun, because in the above story I had only repeated what I heard someone else say concerning God.

In this simple story a basic error happened. I assumed the role of a teacher and spoke words I did not know to be true. This error has been repeated throughout the history of Christianity and no doubt will be repeated in the future. This single event impressed upon me the vital need for Biblical studies. To that end this book is written for all those who have fallen away from the faith because they have never heard the truth.

This book is written to unmask the operation of worry and to set free those who are gripped and unable to function free of worry's control—those who continue to be robbed by worry of the fullness of their life in Christ. As you read these pages, may you truly realize that YOU ARE FREE TO WORRY NO MORE!

William V. McDonald
Austin, Texas
March 1999

Let's Correct Our Thinking
Chapter 1

Today there is a subtle unseen force sweeping across this country and the world, enslaving countless numbers of people from all walks of life. This force is so subtle that I have met individuals who believe they were born with it as part of their behavior pattern. Still others are lured into its power without knowing this force is about to take control of their lives. It is clear that once this force has gained acceptance into its victim's heart, the force has now become master of that life.

The force that I am speaking of is called "worry." Let me take a moment to define this word. According to The American Heritage Dictionary, worry means:

> *To feel uneasy about: be troubled, to pull, bite, or tear at something.*
> *To work under difficulty or hardship; struggle: worried away at a problem.*
> *To cause to feel anxious, distressed or troubled.*
> *To bother; annoy: to grasp and tug at repeatedly.*
> *To touch, press or handle idly: toy with.*
> *The act of worrying or the condition of being worried: mental uneasiness or anxiety.*
> *A source of nagging concern or uneasiness.*

Each day this word is being used without regard for its influence or controlling power.

We wake up in the morning thinking about our worries, or we hear others tell us not to worry, or we tell others not to worry. We go so far as to let advertisers sell their products to us because we desire not to worry about this or that. The thing that saddens me the most is how believers in Jesus—God's saints, pastors, teachers, and evangelists—all use this word "worry" without any regard to its controlling power. As members of God's family, we should be more interested in following his commandments and not letting these ungodly forces control our lives. This book is written to unmask the operation of worry and to set free those who are gripped and unable to function free of worry's control.

The shocking reality is that Christians all over the world are under the control of this powerful force called "worry." Consider the words of Jesus who said:

> *Therefore I say unto you, <u>Take no thought</u> for yourself, what you shall eat, or what you shall drink* (Matthew 6:25, KJV).

> *Therefore I tell you, <u>do not worry</u> about your life, what you will eat or drink; or about your body, what you will wear* (Matthew 6:25, NIV).

Let me clarify these words. As a serious Bible student, one who has learned how to study the text in the original languages, I realize how misleading the English translations can be. I also realize how easily a reader can conclude that he or she has an understanding of the scriptures, and can still be misled.

This study will help you to navigate through these problems that, for the most part, readers of the Bible do not realize exist. Now, I know that is a strong statement, so let me explain. When you read your English translation, many of these words do not convey the same meaning today as in the ancient text. Let me give you an excellent example to establish this point.

Take the English word "truth," which can be found in many passages, both in the New Testament and in the Hebrew Scriptures.

> *For the law was given through Moses; grace and <u>truth</u> came through Jesus Christ* (John 1:17, NIV);

> *I am the way, the <u>truth</u>, and the life* (John 14:6, NIV);

> *But when he, the Spirit of <u>truth</u>, is come, he will guide you into all truth* (John 16:13, NIV).

If you are honest with yourselves, when you read these passages, where the word "truth" is being used, your natural understanding of this word embraces the English definition. It is at this point that we make our first mistake. There is a clear, distinct difference between the word used in the original Hebrew text, and our understanding of the English word "truth."

As an example, the English word "truth" is used in our culture as "honesty, integrity" or simply, "the opposite of falsehood." The word used in the Hebrew Scriptures for "truth" is אמת *e-MET,* and it is defined as "faithfulness, reliability, certainty," and "stability." In order to understand the precise Biblical meaning of the word "truth," let us substitute the above definitions for the English word and see how these passages will read. First, in John 1:17 the text says that:

> For the law was given through Moses; grace and _hon-esty_, or grace and _integrity_, or grace and the _opposite of falsehood_ came through Jesus Christ (John 1:17);

> I am the way, the _honesty_, or the _integrity_, or the _opposite of falsehood_, and the life (John 14:6);

> But when he, the Spirit of _honesty_, of _integrity_, or of the _opposite of falsehood_, is come, he will guide you into all _honesty_, all _integrity_, all the _opposite of falsehood_ (John 16:13).

Well, I think you can see how substituting the definition of our English word "truth" completely divorced us from what these passages wanted to convey in the text. However, taking the same exercise, and placing the English definitions of the Hebrew word אמת _e-MET_ into the same passages, causes something beautiful to happen. Let's see: John 1:17,

> For the law was given through Moses; grace and _faithfulness_, or grace and _reliability_, or grace and _certainty_, or grace and _stability_, came through Jesus Christ (John 1:17).

Wow! It is wonderful to see the scriptures come alive in that manner!

> *I am the way, the <u>faithfulness</u>, the <u>reliability</u>, the <u>certainty</u>, the <u>stability</u>, and the life; no man comes to the Father except through me* (John 14:6).

I know that you are feeling the power of God's word as the Spirit is quickening in your heart that this is a correct interpretation. Think about it—Jesus is saying that He is the faithfulness, the sureness upon which we place all of our trust when we come to the Father.

> *But when he, the Spirit of <u>faithfulness</u>, the Spirit of <u>reliability</u>, the Spirit of <u>certainty</u>, the Spirit of <u>stability</u>, is come, he will guide you into all <u>faithfulness</u>, all <u>reliability</u>, all <u>certainty</u>, all <u>stability</u>, for he shall not speak of himself but whatsoever he shall hear, that shall he speak: and he will show you things to come* (John 16:13).

I can not say it any clearer, and I know that you are able to see how important it is to know the precise meaning of Biblical words.

Now let me digress by introducing you to yet another important Biblical principle that is essential in understanding the operation of the sphere of worry. It is related to the last point about using the precise meaning of God's words. In Matthew 5:19, Jesus said,

> *Anyone who breaks one of the least of these commandments and teaches others to do the same will*

*be called least in the kingdom of heaven, but who-
ever practices and teaches these commands will be
called great in the kingdom of heaven* (NIV).

I remember a few months ago, one of my mentors,
Dr. Roy B. Blizzard, was a guest on a TV program I hosted
called "The Quest." I read this passage and asked him
his interpretation, and he said, "Bill, this is one of the
scariest passages in all of the New Testament."

To understand what Jesus was speaking of when He
said that anyone who breaks one of the least commandments and teaches others to do the same will be least in
the kingdom of heaven, we need to consider what Jesus
said in verses 17 and 18. The text records:

> *Think not that I am come to destroy the law, or the
> prophets: I am not come to destroy, but to fulfill.
> For verily I say unto you, till heaven and earth pass,
> one jot or one tittle shall in no wise pass from the
> law, till all be fulfilled* (KJV).

To destroy the law meant to misinterpret the words
of God. Jesus told his listeners that He did not come to
misinterpret the laws or words of God, and for him to
fulfill the law simply meant giving correct interpretation. Jesus was giving reassurance to His audience that
not only would He not misinterpret God's word, He
would not even misinterpret one jot or tittle (jot = *yod*,
the smallest letter of Hebrew alphabet; tittle = decora-
tive flourish on certain letters). He then addressed his
followers by telling them if anyone breaks or misinterprets one of these commandments, his or her ability to

operate in the work of his kingdom will be least effective. However, to the one who correctly teaches or interprets God's word, his or her effectiveness will be great. Jesus placed a heavy responsibility on the shoulders of those called to teach God's word. Dr. Blizzard was referring to the price a person will pay who misinterprets God's word. They ultimately will give account of their ineffective teachings.

The second part of my digression deals with the expression used by Jesus in the above passage, *"in the kingdom of heaven."* In their book, *Understanding the Difficult Words of Jesus,* David Bivin and Roy Blizzard, Jr. write: The concept of "kingdom" is perhaps the most important spiritual concept in the New Testament. In English or Greek, "kingdom" is never active—it is something static, something to do with territory. But, in Hebrew, "kingdom is active, it is action. It is God ruling in the lives of men. Those who are ruled by God are the kingdom of God. "Kingdom" is also the demonstration of God's rule through miracles, signs, and wonders. Wherever the power of God is demonstrated, there is His "kingdom." Jesus also used "kingdom" to refer to those who followed Him, the members of His movement. His disciples were now to literally be the kingdom of God by demonstrating His presence and power in their lives. (Bivin and Blizzard. p. 64)

Jesus' point in Matthew 5:19 was that anyone who followed Him and became a teacher of God's word would have great ability to demonstrate the supernatural power of this kingdom if they interpreted the word correctly. However, if anyone misinterpreted the word, his or her effectiveness in the Kingdom of God would be less.

What powerful interpretation of Scripture! As you can see, there is room to learn more about the words of God by turning to the ancient language of Hebrew. Such is the case when we read the words of Jesus in Matthew 6: 25, as He tells his followers not to worry. Scholars today who are studying the Bible using the Hebrew Scriptures, or what we call the Old Testament, are able to examine the words of Jesus in light of his original culture, thus allowing us to hear Jesus almost as if we were standing right there with Him.

So what did Jesus mean when He said, *"Therefore I say unto you do not worry."* I have already given you the English definitions of the word worry. Now let me give you the Biblical word for worry in Hebrew. It is the word דאג *da-AHG* and according to the *Brown-Driver-Briggs Hebrew-English Lexicon* (BDB), this word means: *be anxious, fear, be anxious with reference to, in behalf of: to dread, anxiety, anxious care, anxiety for fear of.* Now in order for me to explain how Jesus is using this word that is translated as *worry* in the NIV and *thought* in the KJV, it is imperative that I set the stage so that you will be able clearly to see the sphere of operation in which this force "worry" exists. To do so means that I must go back to the very beginning of creation, and point out that worry as a spiritual force is a spiritual law created by God. As a spiritual law created by God it can only function within the sphere in which it was given authority to operate.

AN UNSEEN FORCE

CHAPTER 2

This might be somewhat confusing to you so let me build upon the last statement (that worry was created by God) by taking a look at supporting Scriptures. In Colossians 1:9-17 (KJV) we read:

> *For this cause we also, since the day we heard it, do not cease to pray for you, and to desire that ye might be filled with the knowledge of his will in all wisdom and spiritual understanding; That ye might walk worthy of the Lord unto all pleasing, being fruitful in every good work, and increasing in the knowledge of God; Strengthened with all might, according to his glorious power, unto all patience and Longsuffering with joyfulness; Giving thanks unto the Father, which hath made us meet to be partakers of the inheritance of the saints in light Who hath delivered us from the power of darkness, and hath translated us into the kingdom of his dear Son: In whom we have redemption through his blood, even the forgiveness of sins: Who is the image of the invisible God, the firstborn of every creature: For by him were all things created, that are in heaven, and that are in earth, visible and invisible, whether they be thrones, or dominions, or principalities, or powers: all things were created by him, powers, and for him. And he is before all things, and by him all things consist.*

9

Paul the Apostle wrote these words to those followers of Jesus who were in Colosse, telling them more about
who they were in relation to their new lives they now
had in Jesus. In the above passages I selected, Paul tells
his readers that it is his desire that they be filled with
knowledge, wisdom, and spiritual understanding. I think
Paul is about to take his readers into new areas of spiritual life, whereby he might be able to introduce them to
God's higher spiritual laws. He tells them in verse 13
that they have been delivered from the power of darkness and translated into the kingdom of his dear Son.
God's work is complete, and his promises are faithful
and everlasting. God said in this passage that his followers do not have to continue to walk in ways that are
unpleasing to him. Paul is calling his readers to a walk
in spiritual truths whereby they can understand the process of being strengthened with God's glorious power.
Therefore it is your spiritual right to rejoice, for God
surely has made you to be a partaker of his inheritance
with all other saints.

Paul is saying that it does not matter about the spiritual forces that may come against you, the kind you are
unable to see, like worry, for example. Because God told
Paul in verse 16, all things—let me say that again— God
told Paul that **all** things were created by Him. God is
saying whether it is things that operate in the heavens or
things that operate in the earth, still they all were created by him. Just to be emphatic about the matter Paul
writes that even the visible and invisible forces or laws,
*"whether they be thrones, or dominions, or principalities,
or powers,"* were created by him, and for him.

How does worry fit into this picture? Well, worry is a principality, worry is a power or a dominion of the unseen world. Worry is an invisible spiritual force that exists, and therefore, if it exists, it too was created by God. Some of you will have a hard time coming to grips with this point. Nevertheless, if we are to believe the writings of the Apostle Paul, we can only conclude that God is the creator of all invisible forces like worry. If He created worry, and I believe he did, then worry like all other creations of God must have a purpose. As an example, consider the unseen force of gravity. Although we cannot see gravity, we certainly are aware of its existence. Another example can be seen in the law of physics that states that for every action there is an equal and opposite reaction. We also have natural laws that govern the forces that enable electricity to power motors and to produce light. Each of these invisible forces was created by God and since the beginning of creation they have been operating to their purpose. Such is the case with this spiritual force called worry.

Let's take a look at "worry" operating in Scripture. Genesis 4:3-7 (KJV) states:

> *In the course of time Cain brought some of the fruits of the soil as an offering to the Lord. But Abel brought fat portions from some of the firstborn of his flock. The Lord looked with favor on Abel and his offering, but on Cain and his offering he did not look with favor. So Cain was very angry, and his face was downcast. Then the Lord said to Cain, Why are you angry? Why is your face downcast? If you do what is right, will you not be accepted? But*

if you do not do what is right, sin is crouching at your door; it desires to have you, but you must master it.

In examining these passages several basic questions need to be addressed. The text does not tell us why Cain and Abel are making offerings to the Lord. We must assume that God told them what was expected of them. For example in Micah 6:6-8 (NIV) we read:

With what shall I come before the Lord and bow down before the exalted God? Shall I come before him with burnt offerings, with calves a year old? Will the Lord be pleased with thousands of rams, with ten thousand rivers of oil? Shall I offer my firstborn for my transgression, the fruit of my body for the sin of my soul? He has showed you, O man, what is good, And what does the Lord require of you? To act justly and to love mercy and to walk humbly with your God.

It would appear that Abel did what God told him to do and Cain, well, he did not! Because Cain did not do what God told him to do his face became downcast, or as the King James text records it, "his countenance fell."

I can remember during the last school year my 9th-grade son came slowly walking into my room, and as I looked upon his face it was downcast, his countenance had fallen. I knew something was wrong, so I asked. He came closer and he handed me his grade card. The evidence was upon my son's face just as it was upon Cain's face. So God asked Cain, "Why are you worried? Why

are you gripped with anger and anxiety?" ʾ
did what was required of him, and Cain did ⁿ⌐
was worried. Likewise, my son had already begun ⌐
worry when he walked into my room. He was listening
to voices speaking in his mind/heart telling him things
that could possibly happen because of his grades. My
youngest son was being confronted with the conditions
of life. In a similar manner, they will force you to master them or they will work to master you. As for Cain,
he had to deal with almighty God. As for my son, well
at that moment, he had only to deal with me.

That must have been a very uncertain moment for
Cain, not knowing what God would do. And yet, our
loving God gave to Cain a principle in these words: *"If
you do what is right, will you not be accepted?"* "Cain my
son, you don't have to worry about anything. You don't
have to even take thought, my son, because when you
do what is right you will always be accepted" (author's
paraphrase). Glory 2 God! Make a special note here because this is a true principle of God, and one of the most
important steps in learning how to stop worrying. That
step is always to do what is right, and know that God
and the laws He established will produce right back to
you in action or deeds. Let me state this point again:
always do what is right.

The text went on to state that if you don't do what is
right, sin will crouch at your door. Let's examine this
word "sin." The Hebrew noun used in Genesis 4:7 is
חַטָּאת *chat-TAT* sin from the root verb חָטָא *cha-TAH* sin.
This is a verb meaning *to miss (a goal or way), go wrong,
miss the goal or path of right and duty,* or *to miss the mark.*
This word is easy to understand in and of itself; how-

ever, the context of how this word is being used can reveal more by breaking down the word to an even simpler component. We need to ask the question, what is crouching at the door, and what is meant by the door (based upon the above definition of the Hebrew word for sin)? The next question to ask is how sin gets to be sin, and how it relates to crouching at your door?

One of the simplest methods I have used over the years in learning the meaning of a word is to use synonymous terms. Therefore, when the Scriptures speak of sin crouching at the door, it is important to acknowledge that what crouches at our door is the invisible force of sin. I believe the scripture is talking about the door of life at which sin awaits. At the door of life, sin looks for its opportunities. The synonymous words I use for sin are "life" and "problems." The text says that sin crouches at the door. If you choose to give in to sin, if you miss the mark, you become like Cain; however, if you hit the mark by doing what is right, you will be accepted like Abel.

Now let me give you my translation of Genesis 4:7 by using synonymous terms. Consider when God said to Cain, "Why are you crying like a child?" (author's paraphrase) "Don't you know that if you do right, you will be accepted? However, if you do not do what is right", God said, "life, problems, or sin, crouches at your door." Think about what I have just said for a moment—life crouches at your door—problems crouch at your door—sin crouches at your door. Is this not correct? Each day of our life we experience joy, sadness, etc.—you know—the natural conditions each day brings.

Meanwhile, as long as we are alive, life and the conditions that produce sin will be here as well. As you well know, life will provide you with a variety of opportunities or conditions, and some of them produce problems, which produce sin. I can remember many years ago traveling to Peoria where I was speaking in a Church called Agape Fellowship, with Pastors William and Marlo Stewart. It was a Wednesday night service, and during that day I met with some of the members. One after the other talked about problems they were experiencing and it seemed to me that it was not going to end. That night as I stood to teach what was to be a well prepared message, I found myself shouting to the people telling them to "stop your complaining about problems!" I asked by show of hands if there was anyone in the Church that night, from the oldest to the youngest, who could raise his or her hand to indicate he or she no longer experienced any problems. No one responded. The simple truth of the matter is that problems are an ever-present reality of life.

Without my knowing at that time, a simple principle was being birthed in my heart, spirit, mind. The principle was that life will bring opportunities, and place them at the door of our lives. We are then confronted with the task of choosing to do right or to do wrong. If you choose wrong, the opportunity that crouches at your door becomes a problem and the wrong choice becomes sin. This sequence is one of the natural courses of life. We do not control whether life will set problems at our door or not. What we can control is our ability to choose what is right or wrong.

Here is another very important point you need to learn about the operation of worry! First, worry is an unseen spiritual force created by God and given the authority by God to present its sphere of operation at the door of your being. The vehicle which worry uses to gain entrance through your heart's door will center around problems you are experiencing. Let me be very practical in illustrating this process.

You get a phone call and learn a loved one has been in a car accident. Life has presented you with one of its problems. Because it is a loved one, immediately your emotions flare up. The only information you have is that your loved one was in the accident. Worry steps up, and seizes the opportunity by piggybacking onto the situation. It begins by suggesting to you possible conditions your loved one might be experiencing. Note that a suggestion is presented to you without your knowing the answer. At this moment, worry is only an unseen spiritual force trying to entice you. Worry cannot become worry until you choose to accept one of its many conditions being presented to your mind. Let me point something out to you here: worry is now in direct contact with your mind, heart, spirit, your very being. At this point you will begin to hear and see word pictures in your mind. These pictures are about your loved one, and worry is trying to pull you further into its control. I will return to this point later.

Genesis 4:7 says that חטא cha-TAH sin desires to have you. Again, sin is not some type of independent force operating free from the control of God. After all, God created elements of sin, as He created all things. Therefore, it stands to reason that if God created sin, He also gave sin a purpose and function. One large part of sin's purpose and function was to crouch at our door. Sin will work at enticing us in order *"to have you."* The fact of the matter is that the spiritual laws of sin will pursue you throughout all of your life on earth. The last part of verse 7 is the most important part. It says, *"but you must master it."* Let me go back to the word *"desires,"* and to the words *"to have you"* before concluding this passage. Desire is a very strong component. It deals with the physical and emotional makeup of a being. Desire does not conclude which course of action you will take. Desire only stimulates the force within you to long for, or to crave, sometimes in an uncontrollable manner. Herein desire is another element which God said you should be mastering.

It is interesting that *"to have you"* is the Hebrew word אליך transliterated into English as *ey-LAY-kah*. The King James Version translates this part of verse 7 as *"unto thee shall be his desire."* Whatever this *ey-LA Y-kah* (to have you) is, it operates in both the visible and invisible realm. According to BDB, *ey-LAY-kah* has to do with motion or direction toward, and that motion can be physical or mental.

YOU MUST MASTER IT
CHAPTER 3

In Cain's case, God was telling him that the circumstances of life led him to have a downcast face. Those conditions that caused Cain to have a downcast face, were the unseen forces created by God. These unseen spiritual forces were given the authority and the function to move toward a person either physically or mentally. Think about what I have just said. In order to learn how to control your ability not to worry, you need to understand the sphere in which these forces operate. Worry, as an unseen force, can also be defined as a law, like the Law of Gravity. When God created this world, we know that He established laws. In Christianity we think of these laws as the Ten Commandments, and in the Jewish teachings there are 613 Commandments of God's laws.

I want to add that there are other unseen laws created by God and given specific purpose by God to operate in this sphere in which we live. That is to say, I believe there are many unseen Laws interacting with the choices we make each hour, each day. I am sure you understand that the law of gravity was not created at the moment Newton was sitting under the tree and this apple dropped, hitting him on the head according to the legend. No, of course not! Newton became aware of a law which had existed from the foundation of this world, and which was created by God when the world was

created. However, because of Newton we now understand about the pull that gravity has on the earth, and
we also have learned how not to violate this law for obvious reasons. And yet, because of our lack of knowledge, we are violating other unseen laws that are interacting with us each and every day. It is these violations
we encounter each day which allows a force like worry
to enter our being, and to control who we are, sometimes without us knowing it.

In Genesis 4:7, after God clearly pointed out the pit-
falls before Cain, He spoke to him about the authority
He has given him to rule over all the conditions of life.
God simply said, *"you must master it."* Glory 2 God!
What powerful words spoken by God, "you must master it." This statement is two-fold in nature: first, you
have experienced life's problems in ways that left you
knowing that you personally do not have the answer to
mastering all life's problems.

Second, because we are unable to master life's problems, a spiritual force like worry will take advantage of
our weakness and become a stronghold in our life. In
order for us to master life's problems we are going to
need some type of spiritual help. Because we are unaware of God's principles which govern the spritual forces
like worry, those forces will exert their uninvited influence in our life. So the big question becomes, "God,
how do we master sin, life's problems and worry?" The
answer lies within these spoken words of God, "You must
master it." The authority to fulfill God's promise is in
those words He has spoken. Now, if you are at the point
where you are willing to ask this question, "What is next,
God?" then you are ready to learn, because the One who
created worry is also the One who will teach you how to
master it.

Did Saul's Father Worry?
Chapter 4

Let us develop the operation of worry contextually looking into the Scriptures. In the story found in 1 Samuel chapter nine, where Samuel anoints Saul, we learn that donkeys belonging to Kish, Saul's father, were lost. Kish tells Saul to take one of their servants and go find the donkeys. The text tells us that Saul and the servant passed through the hill country of Ephraim and Shalisha, and they did not find the donkeys. They continued through the territory of Benjamin, and still they did not find the donkeys. After they had reached the district of Zuph, Saul said to the servant,

> *Come, let's go back, or my father will stop thinking about the donkeys and start worrying about us* (1 Samuel 9:5, NIV).

> *Let us return; lest my father leave caring for the asses, and take thought for us* (1 Samuel 9:5, KJV).

In this Bible story it would seem that Saul is concerned that Kish, his father, might be overtaken with worry. Well, the servant with Saul suggested that they enter the nearby city and call upon the man of God there for assistance in finding the donkeys. Little did Saul know when he set out to find the lost donkeys, and felt that his father was about to take thought or worry about him, that it would become a journey that would lead him toward his destiny. The prophet of whom the servant spoke was Samuel, and according to the text, on the day before Saul and his servant reached the village where Samuel was, God told Samuel that a man from the land of Benjamin would come to him. This man (Saul) was to become the leader over God's people Israel, and Samuel was to anoint him. This story is very interesting because right in the midst of a natural condition of life (problems crouching at the door of Kish), God Himself had chosen Saul to deliver His people from the hand of the Philistines.

Thank God for Kish's servant, because Saul was probably feeling the same anxiety, fear, and worry his father felt. The story tells us that Saul was ready to turn around and head home. Right now there are many of God's people who feel this same invisible force of worry pulling at their hearts. It is telling them to turn around, telling them that they cannot master the problems of life, telling them how they now have lost their way, and telling them this task is too great for them to master. So we take thought, give in to the voice of worry, and become a slave to forces that were created to be mastered by us. However, Kish's servant was not under the personal strain that Saul felt; he suggested that they go ahead to the next city.

> *When Samuel caught sight of Saul, the Lord said to him, 'This is the man I spoke to you about; he will govern my people'"* (1 Samuel 9:17, NIV).

In chapter ten, Samuel said that the Lord had anointed Saul to be leader over His inheritance, and that when he left to return home he would find the two donkeys. Samuel also told him that his father was no longer thinking about the two donkeys; he was now worried about his son.

So here we have a scenario in which what begins as a work related task results in a cause for worry. Kish sent Saul and a servant to find two donkeys. They traveled a great distance from home, which took a few days. Saul's father was unaware of what was happening to his son. All he knew was that Saul and a servant had been away from home for over two days. Meanwhile Samuel, the prophet, said to Saul that Saul's father was no longer worrying about his donkeys, but had now begun to worry about him. I would think the same degree of concern Kish had for Saul, we also have for our loved ones when in similar situations.

When Jesus said, "Don't even take thought!" (author's paraphrase), He knew all about this unseen force, this invisible law created by God, lurking about or crouching at the door of life. Jesus knew that this creative force called worry, which is the Hebrew word דאג (da-AHG), would make attempts at enticing the mind of anyone who would receive its efforts. In the case of Kish, Saul's father, he took thought (worried) about his son.

Let me give you an example of taking thought or worry: Worry might have suggested these options to the mind of Kish: "Your son has been taken by a band of robbers, or maybe he has been injured, or has been killed by animals." The fact is that there were many situations in which Kish could have taken thought or worried about his son. And yet, something much more profound was happening to his son while Kish was giving in to worry. God was fulfilling the destiny of Saul right in the midst of anxiety, uncertainty, and, yes, in the midst of worry.

For your reference, you can find the Hebrew word דאג (da-AHG) used in Isaiah 57:11; Jeremiah 38:19; Jeremiah 42:16; and in Psalm 38:18, where the NIV says:

> *For I am about to fall, and my pain is ever with me. I confess my iniquity; I am troubled by my sin.*

The KJV used the words "my sorrow is continually before me." Both the NIV and the KJV are translating the Hebrew words אדאג מחטאתי (literally, "I am *worried* by my sin"). The English text used the words *sorrow* and *troubled*, but the Psalmist was expressing the heaviness of his heart, as in verse 13 and 14 (NIV):

> *I am like a deaf man, who cannot hear, like a mute, who cannot open his mouth, I have become like a man who does not hear, whose mouth can offer no reply.*

Why? Because worry was gripping his heart/mind/ spirit, and worry was controlling everything he heard. His sins, or might I say, his doing what was wrong, opened the door to the powerful influence of the voice of worry. Still the Psalmist cried out in verse 22, *"Come quickly to help me, 0 Lord my Savior."*

In Jeremiah Chapter 17, he speaks of the sins of Judah and how they were engraved on the tablets of the hearts of the people. Jeremiah speaks of a heavy price for sin that the people were about to pay. He told them that God would enslave them by turning them over to their enemies, and letting them be taken to a land they did not know. Think about this condition: the people of Judah had become more wicked than their fathers, who also had disobeyed God. They had chosen to follow other gods by serving and worshipping them. Jeremiah reminded the people of Judah about what was required of them in verse seven, "...blessed is the man who trusts in the Lord, whose confidence is Him"(NIV). Then Jeremiah used a metaphor to express the safety, the faithfulness, the certainty that the people could have experienced had they obeyed God. In verse eight, Jeremiah wrote:

> He will be like a tree planted by the water that sends out its roots by the stream. It does not fear when heat comes; its leaves are always green. It has no worries in a year of drought and never fails to bear fruit (NIV).

Wow, let us examine this text! Two times the text speaks of our subject, worry, together with fear. The prophet spoke of a coming doom which the people were destined to face, a condition which had to cause a tremendous amount of worry in the hearts of the people. It would seem as if Jeremiah reinforced the words of God recorded in Genesis 4:7 where God said, "If you do what is right you will be accepted." Jeremiah wanted Judah to know that there would be no worries if they did what was right. He told them that they could be like the tree that is planted by the water. The people would not be experiencing fear, and thereby there would be no need for a coming punishment of God. If only they had sent out their roots of obedience to the stream of their ever faithful God. Jeremiah wanted them to know that it did not matter how hot the conditions of life got in times of lack or drought, because their God was the one who feeds the birds of the air, and provides water for the trees. The words of Jeremiah are consistent with the words spoken by Jesus:

> *Behold the fowls of the air: for they sow not, neither do they reap, nor gather into barns. yet your heavenly Father feedeth them. Are ye not much better than they?"* (Matthew 6:26, KJV).

WORRY AND ITS OPERATIONS
CHAPTER 5

Today, with all the heaviness of life's pressures and the uncertainties of each day, how can a child of God truly live his or her life and not worry? Well, before I answer this question it is important for me to take you on another journey—a journey that I believe will open your hearts to a better understanding of God's purpose for all mankind. That of which I am about to inform you will help you to see worry in its operation, and to place it in a sphere where you can see just how God gives His people authority over it and all other unseen forces.

This journey also begins in the book of Genesis, in chapter one with what I call the Creative Order of God where God creates the universe. In Genesis we read: 1:3ff.(KJV): *"And God said, 'Let there be light, and there was light.'"* Take a moment and think about this statement. In all of our acquired knowledge today I have yet to see or hear of any person who has or has had the ability to speak and have what he or she says to come into existence. God did! God can! Glory! God said:

> *Let there be a firmament in the midst of the waters, and let it divide the waters from the waters: and it was so.*
> *Let the water under the heaven be gathered together unto one place and let the dry land appear.*

Let the earth bring forth grass, the herb yielding seed, and the fruit tree yielding fruit after his kind: and it was so.
Let the earth bring forth the living creature after his kind, cattle, and creeping thing, and beast of the earth after his kind: and it was so.

God simply spoke, and the power that is within His words caused His words to manifest bringing the unseen into existence. What an awesome display of the nature and character of our God! With just a spoken word God created things which were not, and they became so. In Genesis 1:26 (author's paraphrase) God again said:

Let us make mankind in our image, after our likeness: and let them have dominion over all the creative order of this world.

Now dear child of God, I ask you, why have these powerful creative words of God not become so in us? God Himself said that mankind was created in His image and likeness, and I ask you, "Can we say that we know of any man or woman who reflects the total image and likeness of God on this earth?" The fact is that the only one who has ever lived and reflected the totality of all that God is, was Jesus. Thank you God!

Everything that God said or spoke became so. Yet when we look at ourselves, we cannot say we reflect the fullness of God. You may say the reason is because of the fall of Adam and Eve. They altered the plan of God by sinning; therefore, God had to come up with a plan to redeem His creation, mankind. I don't believe it! I believe the God we serve, who we call the all-seeing and all-knowing God, knew the actions and thoughts of the hearts of His creation from the very beginning. I seriously doubt that God was surprised by Adam and Eve's choice. The fact of the matter is, God knew what their actions would be just as He knows our actions today.

Many years ago while in seminary, I can remember a course that was more practical than academic. In that course we covered the Genesis account of Adam's and Eve's fall. The dominant theology being taught was that after the fall, God had to come up with another plan for mankind. You might have heard of this theology, too. Well I had problems with that interpretation then and I have problems with it now. In my pursuit of learning about God, it was and still is important for me to find a consistency in and with God. When I heard the professor state that God had to come up with another plan, I saw a God who was not all-knowing, a God who was not all-seeing. That was not the God I held in my heart—the God whose ways were higher than ours, and whose thoughts were higher than ours. It just could not be the same God who spoke and a universe was created, a God who would later learn that He had to come up with another plan because His crown of creation had failed. This position just did not make sense!

For a while there was an emptiness in my heart, because I did not have the answer and I was not about to settle for what I had been told about the fall of Adam and Eve. Then I read two passages that revolutionized my thinking. Revelation 13:8 (KJV):

And all that dwell upon the earth shall worship him, whose names are not written in the book of life of the Lamb slain from the foundation of the world.

Glory 2 God! Then I read in I Peter 1:18-20 (KJV):

For you know that it was not with perishable things such as silver or gold that you were redeemed from the empty way of life handed down to you from your forefathers, but with the precious blood of Christ, a lamb without blemish or defect He was chosen before the creation of the world.

Hallelujah! Before He created the world, God chose Jesus to be a perfect sacrifice for all mankind. That told me that God knew just what Adam and Eve were going to do, and His plan was and is consistent from the start to the end.

One more piece of supporting evidence that God knew what Adam and Eve were going to do is found in Genesis 2:17. Now I know that you may not be able to read Hebrew. However, it is important for you to know and understand that the Hebrew passage of this verse is being translated as literally as possible.

ומעץ הדעת טוב ורע לא תאכל ממנו כי ביום אכלך
ממנו מות תמות:

And from tree the knowledge of good and evil, not you shall eat; for in the day you eat from it, surely you shall die.

30

If you check your Bible you will see that the text states the same thing. It said *"in the day that you eat,"* which implies that God knew that they would eat. Now, if God did not have knowledge of what Adam and Eve were going to do, the text could have read:

> *...but the tree of knowledge of good and evil, you shall not eat. But if you choose to eat from it, in that day you shall surely die.*

Truly, the God who spoke and a world was created could have stated clearly what He understood or did not understand. Whether or not Adam and Eve were going to eat of the forbidden fruit, I believe God knew, and that is why the text states: *"...for in the day you eat from it, you shall surely die."*

Let me return to the question I asked earlier, which was, "Why is mankind not reflecting the same image and likeness of God? After all, the Scriptures teach us that we were made in His image and likeness, and the Scriptures teach us that everything that was declared from the mouth of God became so. We can see the evidence of the work of God. We can see the light that became known as day and we can see the darkness that became known as night. We can see the stars in the heavens, and we can see the living things reproducing after its kind. However, what about mankind? Why do we not see him living and having dominion over all of the creation of God?" This is an important question, because in Isaiah 55:10-11 (KJV) the text states:

31

For as the rain cometh down, and the snow from heaven, and returneth not thither, but watereth the earth, and maketh it bring forth and bud, that it may give seed to the sower, and bread to the eater: So shall my word be that goeth forth out of my mouth: it shall not return unto me void, but it shall accomplish that which I please, and it shall prosper in the thing whereto I sent it.

Therefore, if God said that mankind was and is made in His image and likeness and given the authority to have dominion over all of that which God created, I ask again, "Why is it not so?" Well, Glory 2 God, I believe it is still so and that those words have the same authority now as they did then! In Isaiah, God said that His word will not return to Him void or return to Him unfulfilled. God spoke and said that mankind was made in His image and likeness, with the authority to have dominion over the entire world. It is clear that mankind is not walking or living in that authority, nor having dominion over all of God's creation. So the big question is, "Where are these words which God spoke in Genesis 1:26 and 27?" These words have not been fulfilled in mankind and they surely have not returned to God, so where are these unfulfilled words of God? It is at this point that I want to introduce you to my understanding about how God has given us a plan whereby we can be transformed into His image and likeness. Paul called it "being renewed in our mind."

32

You Must Be Transformed
Chapter 6

I believe the words God spoke concerning mankind in Genesis 1:26 are in the spiritual realm, and in the spiritual realm they await all who would climb up to where God is and lay hold of what He has given us. I believe an unseen realm exists where God intended His creation, mankind, to reflect the totality of all that He is. In that spiritual realm we can receive, and reflect the total image and likeness of our God. One of our greatest errors is that we diminish God's nature in judging God by the actions of man. My personal observation is that the human species is bent on lowering his or her expectations, thereby lowering the standards of God. Let me explain more about how we lower the standards of God in our human actions.

We start out by taking the awesome power and authority of God's word, and water it down with interpretations that fit our personal preference. We look for ways where we can outwardly appear to be embracing God's words while inwardly we are giving in to the weaknesses of our emotions. We choose to wear Christian pins on our lapels or to place the fish sign on our cars, instead of letting the light that Jesus spoke of in Matthew 5:14 shine before men. The simple truth of the matter is that we do not know how to be the salt or light of the world. Therefore, the high standards that are within God's words are lowered to levels whereby our

outward actions are allowing us to feel as if we are living
by God's words. This simplifies life, as we attempt to
remove the responsibility of God's high standards from
our shoulders. You see, the level of existence by which
God has ordained all to live places the responsibility of
His standards squarely upon our shoulders. Again, instead of striving to master life as God told Cain in Genesis 4:7, we, on the other hand, choose to give in to spiritual forces like worry and fear. By not ruling or having
dominion over our emotions, we are surrendering to
unseen forces like worry and fear our God-given authority and creativity to master life problems. Yes, I believe
that God proclaimed that mankind was made in His
image and likeness and I believe that Adam and Eve ate
of the tree. However, the fall of Adam and Eve did not
change the creative plan of God. The fact is that the
authority established in God's word did not and will
not return to Him unfulfilled. The commandment given
to Adam to have dominion over all the earth exists in a
spiritual realm, because any words spoken by God will
not return to Him unfulfilled. God has left it up to mankind (you and me) to reach up to this spiritual level
whereby we can fulfill this promise or commandment
of God. In fact, Genesis 5:24 speaks of Enoch who
walked with God, and because of his obedience *"he did
not die but God took him away"*(KJV). The name Enoch
in Hebrew is חנוך *ha-NOK*, which comes from the root
word in Hebrew חנך *ha-NAK*. According to BDB, the
root word means "to train up, to dedicate," as in Proverbs 22:6,

> *Train up a child in the way he should go: and when
> he is old, he will not depart from it* (KJV).

God spoke these words in Proverbs and commanded His people to do what He had said, but also to teach His commandments to their children. The interesting thing about this passage is that because God said these words there must be a way in which we His people can do what He said. Jesus reached that level, and He calls each of us to do the same. God has placed us in a world in which we can experience challenges that can shape and mold our nature into His nature. When we live in this world with non-renewed minds and spirits, we are living as though we want to stay in the darkness instead of coming into His light.

Now Jesus is pointing you to this higher realm where the word of God spoken in Genesis 2:26 is waiting to be fulfilled in your life. It is this spiritual realm in which God wants you to enter into His peace and His joy, and never have to take thought or worry or fear about anything in life. It is the same spiritual realm where God told Cain he had to master life. The question Cain needed to ask then, and which we need to ask today is, "God, how do I master life?"

Let's further develop this concept in which you are being called to reach up to the level where God has placed the authority whereby you can begin to master life. And yes, that means mastering worry. I want you to think about what the Bible calls "strongholds"—anything that has become a controlling factor in your life. 2 Corinthians 10:3-5 (KJV) says,

> For though we walk in the flesh, we do not war after the flesh: For the weapons of our warfare are not carnal, but mighty through God to the pulling down of strongholds: Casting down imaginations,

35

and every high thing that exalteth itself against the knowledge of God, and bringing into captivity every thought to the obedience of Christ.

Worry is one of those high things, an unseen spiritual force that exalts itself against the will of God.

I can remember many years ago when there were lots of strongholds in my life. One such stronghold for me was this unseen spiritual force called worry. Worry was so much a part of my life that when worry presented itself to me, I was unaware I had taken thought and unaware I was worrying. I, like so many others, felt that worry was a natural part of my life. It was not until I read these words of Jesus that I began to think about not worrying: *"Therefore I tell you, do not worry about your life"* (Matthew 6:25, NIV). For the first time I began to question worry as a part of my life. And because I wanted to please God with all my heart, I can remember praying, "God please help me to learn how not to worry any more."

It was an early time of growing in God for me, and I was learning how to trust God's words. To my joy, the answer was right there in the word of God all the time. When I read God's word it was as if Jesus Himself was speaking directly to me, telling me, "William, you don't have to worry any more." I did not know how to stop worrying at that time. However, I knew God's word was to be trusted more than the worry that was controlling me. (Let me also say that another important factor in my overcoming worry centered around "faith," a subject I will address shortly.) So I promised myself I would stop worrying, and, you know, I truly wanted to stop.

By this time, however, worry had become the master of my life, and I could do nothing about its control. In spite of the fact that I promised myself I would stop worrying, it seemed as if worry would not take my promise seriously. Because worry as a spiritual force was controlling my emotions, worry was controlling my life.

Think about how many times you have promised yourself and others that you were going to stop letting strongholds control your life. Think about what has been the result of your promises. If you are like me, your promises have ended with you failing over and over again. The law of worry is a spiritual law like the unseen law of gravity. When you exercise your free will and choose to worry, you have given access to the powers of worry and permitted them to operate in your life. That is why the more you try to stop worrying, the stronger worry gets in your life.

This is a very interesting point. When we reach a point of complete weakness, and when we are able to acknowledge that we are no longer in control, that is the moment God is ready to touch us the strongest. I believe that at this time something beautiful is about to be released in us. Paul called it "transformation," and it is a time when Romans 8:28, And we know that all things work together for good to them that love God, to them who are the called according to his purpose (KJV) can, and will work the most effectively. Let me give you an example from the text to establish the point I am making here. In II Chronicles chapter 20, King Jehoshaphat and the people of Judah were facing the mighty armies of the Moabites, Ammonites and some of the Meunites.

In verses 15 to 17 (NIV) the text says,

> He said: 'Listen, King Jehoshaphat and all who live
> in Judah and Jerusalem! This is what the Lord says
> to you: Do not be afraid or discouraged because of
> this vast army. For the battle is not yours, but God's.
> Tomorrow march down against them. They will be
> climbing up by the Pass of Ziz, and you will find
> them at the end of the gorge in the Desert of Jeruel.
> You will not have to fight this battle. Take up your
> positions; stand firm and see the deliverance the Lord
> will give you, O Judah and Jerusalem. Do not be
> afraid; do not be discouraged. Go out to face them
> tomorrow, and the Lord will be with you.

Wow, what a wonderful promise God gave His
people! Would it not be wonderful if God were saying
to you, "Do not be afraid or discouraged because of worry
for the battle is not yours." Rest assured, my brother
and sister, it is indeed His will to set you free from worry.

In II Chronicles chapter 20, we have an excellent example of how God dealt with the people as a nation
rather than individually. In this situation the people
were confronted with enemies over whom they knew
they could not gain victory. There are situations like
this one recorded throughout the Hebrew Scriptures,
where God's people faced battles against armies or enemies they simply could not defeat. The enemies of
Judah were the hostile armies, while the enemies with
which you and I must deal can be any stronghold such
as that of worry. King Jehoshaphat, speaking for the
people, in verse 12 declared, "...for we have no power to

face this vast army that is attacking us. We do not know what to do, but our eyes are upon You" (NIV). God wants His people to know that He and He alone is their deliverer. In the history of the people of Israel and Judah, there were many situations in which the people found themselves facing enemies that they could not defeat. Time and time again God delivered the Israelites from their enemies. The conditions they faced were of such hoplessness that no one could take credit for the coming victory except God. Because of God's mighty redeeming hand even the enemies of Israel knew that these people served a God of power and authority.

This is a very important point. The people of Israel were faced with a stronghold. Their stronghold was the other nations about to overtake them in battle. The people knew without a doubt they could not overcome the forces confronting them at the moment, much like the conditions that we face with worry. Worry, as a stronghold, will present its many options to you. If you choose any of worry's options, the journey has begun and worry is on its way toward mastering you. Therefore, like the people of Israel, you are in need of God's redeeming love. The fact is, once worry gains access into your being, it is very difficult to stop it from controlling your emotions and thus, your life.

As a follower of Christ it is imperative that we learn to embrace Paul's teachings concerning being transformed by the renewing of our minds. Romans 12:1-2 (NIV) states:

> *Therefore, I urge you, brothers, in view of God's mercy, to offer your bodies as living sacrifices, holy*

and pleasing to God—this is your spiritual act of worship. Do not conform any longer to the pattern of this world. But be transformed by the renewing of your mind. Then you will be able to test and approve what God's will is—his good, pleasing and perfect will.

The reason I interject this text here is to point out how our day-to-day experiences can sometimes parallel that of the children of Israel. Their enemies presented problems that they could not defeat without God. Under those conditions the Israelites must have felt the force of worry crouching at their door. In the Hebrew Scriptures, God dealt with the people as a nation, i.e., as a nation they rejoiced in blessings, as a nation they were punished, and as a nation they atoned for their sins.

When Jesus became the perfect sacrifice, He opened the spiritual doors for God to deal with His people individually. Through Jesus, God no longer dealt with His people as a nation. This point I am sure most of you already understand. I believe you also understand that because of Jesus, God is dealing with us individually, rather than as a nation. When we are confronted with the pressures of life, like worry, you must understand that an enemy is at work trying to control you totally. The conditions we face are much like those of the people of Israel and Judah with their enemies about to defeat them. God is ready to teach you the most intimate lessons of your life. Note that I used the word "lessons" implying a process that will repeat itself over and over again.

You see, after God delivered Israel from their enemies, the people worshipped God because He had moved on their behalf in an intimate way. They worshipped Him because they knew that God had given them victory over their enemies. Today, in your life, worry is like an enemy whose function is to steal, to kill, and to destroy your life. Israel knew God was their redeemer in spite of the elements of evil working to master their beings. Worry is having success in our lives because of two things. First, worry masters your life because you open the door and let worry into your being. And second, worry masters you because you are still living life by conforming to the patterns of this world. Now, let me explain these two statements. Some of you might be saying, I have not opened the door, nor am I conforming any longer to the patterns of this world.

DON'T CONFORM ANYMORE
CHAPTER 7

I can remember many years ago when my children were growing up at home. My older son, who is now 28, was just beginning to come home at later times. I remember those days so clearly, when he would tell his mother and me that he would be home after the game at 11:00 p.m. At eleven I would be looking for him to enter our home, but if he was not home, well, it was ok for a few minutes. The later it got, however, the more worried I became.

Worry was functioning just as it was created by God to function. The moment my son left the house worry began to speak to my mind telling me things that were going to happen to him. Somehow I moved my mind past those unpleasant thoughts. Worry as a spiritual force was crouching at my door, lurking about, waiting to see when I was going to open the door of my mind/spirit to its influence. It did not matter that I had rejected the first few attempts worry made to gain access into my mind. The reality was, worry was knocking at my door, and I was not prepared to deal with it.

It was 11:30 p.m., and we didn't have any idea where our son was! All we knew was that he was late. Worry also had grown stronger, and because of the weakness of our emotions, the spiritual door, to our hearts was open to worry's operations. The first thing worry did was to flash a number of different possible conditions our son might be confronting. Note this important point: the way worry operates is that after worry flashes pictures before your mind, it then waits for you to choose one of its many negative elements. Once I choose, i.e., take thought, from any of the possible negative pictures being flashed in my mind, worry is now taking me on its journey to its next step. For example, let us say the thought occurred to me that my son and his friend might have been in a car accident. The moment I accepted this thought, worry began to show me pictures of what that accident might look like. By this time I would be in the grasp of worry and be unable to function normally.

At the first level, worry attempts to gain access into your being by presenting you with a number of possible choices. To stop the attacks of worry Jesus said don't take thought; however, I am telling you that in my case the process was on its way. Because I had taken thought or opened the door of my spirit, worry had taken me to its second level and was preparing to control me totally. Worry was now ready to introduce me to its first cousin, "fear." In level two, worry flashed many pictures into my mind. Let's say that I chose the picture that showed my son and his friend had been in a car accident and that my son had a head injury. In my mind I could see the picture so clearly that my emotions were reaching another level. The door of my heart was open, and as I looked upon this dreadful sight, fear walked right in, telling me that my son was dying. Can you see how this unseen spiritual force called worry operates? It was 11:45 p.m. my son was still not home, and the picture that worry was showing me seemed to be so real now. It was 12:30 p.m. Still no word from my son and worry was taking me to level four. As I contemplated the conditions around me and of my son, worry introduced me to another of his first cousins, "depression." Worry, anxiety, fear, and now I was beginning to feel the spirit of depression entering my heart. All of this because I did a very simple thing. I took thought! Yes, I opened the door of my spirit by accepting the thought, and worry, anxiety, fear, and depression came rushing in as if they owned the house of my being.

Some of you believe that because you are Christians, you are no longer conforming to the patterns of this world as Paul states in Roman 12. Unfortunately, each day we often conform more to this world than we conform to God's kingdom. I am unable to express the frustration I feel each day as I watch God's people conforming to this world. It might surprise some of you to read this statement, but I am speaking from personal experience as well as from my observations. The fact is that during those earlier years of my Christian life, I worried. I was a Spirit-filled, Bible-carrying, God-loving Christian—and yes, Jesus was and is my Savior. Yet I still was conforming to the patterns of this world more than I was being transformed into God's kingdom.

FAITH OVERCOMES WORRY

CHAPTER 8

Now that I have unmasked the work of this unseen spiritual force called worry, let me return to Jesus' words found in Matthew 6:25-33 (KJV). The text records:

Therefore I say unto you, take no thought for your life, what ye shall eat, or what ye shall drink: nor yet for your body, what ye shall put on. Is not the life more than meat, and the body than raiment? Behold the fowls of the air:for they sow not, neither do they reap, nor gather into barns; yet your heavenly Father feedeth them. Are you not much better than they? Which of you by taking thought can add one cubit unto his stature? And why take ye thought for raiment? Consider the lilies of the field, how they grow; they toil not, neither do they spin. And yet I say unto you, that even Solomon in all his glory was not arrayed like one of these. Wherefore, if God so clothe the grass of the field, which today is; and tomorrow is cast into the oven, shall he not much more clothe you, 0 ye of little faith? Therefore take no thought saying, "What shall we eat?" or, "What shall we drink?" or, "Wherewithal shall we be clothed?" For after all these things do the Gentiles seek: for your heavenly Father knoweth that ye have need of all these things. But seek ye first the King-

dom of God, and his righteousness; and all these
things shall be added unto you.

I highlighted the words, O you of little faith, because
faith is one of the key elements in mastering worry and
all other spiritual forces. Now before I speak to you
about faith, let me use 2 Thessalonians 1:3-5 (KJV) to
introduce faith and how faith overcomes worry. The
text reads:

> *We are bound to thank God always for you, breth-*
> *ren, as it is meet, because that your faith groweth*
> *exceedingly, and the charity of every one of you all*
> *toward each other aboundeth; So that we ourselves*
> *glory in you in the churches of God for your pa-*
> *tience and faith in all your persecutions and tribu-*
> *lations that you endure: Which is a manifest token*
> *of the righteous judgment of God, that you may be*
> *counted worthy of the kingdom of God, for which*
> *you also suffer.*

This passage says that Paul was duty-bound to thank God,
because those who were a part of the Church grew exceedingly in their faith. Then Paul used a parallel: he
placed patience and faith together telling the Church that
he gloried in their patience and faith, in all their persecutions and tribulations.

Several years ago I chose the above text for a teaching on the subject of "The Creative Order of this World."
The subject was designed to teach that within the creation of God, nothing created by God that we encounter in life should rule or master us. It is important for us

to put God's order first in all we do. After all, God created this world for our purpose, for us to rule, and for us to subdue by having dominion. The text also teaches that the elements of life, like worry, are for the benefit of mankind. Paul, no doubt, was telling the Church at Thessalonica that they were doing a good job in dealing with the conditions of life, like worry, with which they were constantly being bombarded.

Is that not what we need to have in our lives today—to know we are moving beyond our fears, our worries, our difficulties? As I travel from church to church teaching about these principles of God, I am greatly saddened. I want so much to see God's people ruling in life, and reflecting the image and likeness of God in all they do. That is not the case, and so we must be honest with ourselves in order to change. The process in called "transformation." Note this—THERE IS NO EXCEPTION!

I was on a trip to Long Island New York and Baltimore teaching that life's problems are nothing more than **a manifest token of the righteous judgment of God, that you may be counted worthy of the kingdom of God.** I was teaching that the problems of life exist as part of God's overall purpose and because they (problems) crouch at the door of our life, their functions (when we choose one or all of them) will naturally bring us to seeing our utter weakness. However, when we reach that point of being totally helpless, I believe God will use those unseen forces to open the door of our being whereby He can now raise us up to the highest level of reflecting His image and likeness in life. This was and is God's plan from the beginning as recorded in Genesis chapter one. If we choose to follow God's plan for our life, we will master life. But if we do not choose to follow God's plan, then the elements of life, like worry and fear, will master us. We attain the reflection of God's image and likeness by way of "transformation." The laws that govern God's kingdom and the laws that govern the unseen forces of evil are always at work. One important fact is that you are going to be transformed by the laws of evil or you are going to be transformed by the laws of God's kingdom. Again, let me say: THERE IS NO EXCEPTION!

Yes, it is true; you can become the reflection and likeness of God in this world, and, yes, I believe it is the purpose of God for you to do so. However, this process of becoming the reflection and likeness of God is the greatest challenge we face. Paul writes in 2 Corinthians 3:18 (NIV) that:

> *We who with unveiled faces all reflect the Lord's glory, are being transformed into his likeness with ever-increasing glory, which comes from the Lord, who is the Spirit.*

Why, Paul, why is it that we who confess to follow Jesus must be transformed, and how can we be transformed?

The answer to these two questions is found in the reality of who and what we truly are as followers of our King Jesus. The simple fact of the matter is that He left you and me a powerful legacy, a legacy that granted and guaranteed us the ability to rise to the highest level of godly life. It is a legacy that enables us to transcend the natural laws that govern this world. One of those natural laws governing this world is the unseen force of worry. And we must also acknowledge that this powerful legacy, handed down almost two thousand years ago, is operating at one of its lowest levels in history. Aside from the Church's dynamic ability to evangelize, the body of Christ is functioning at a level so low that it brings pain to my heart thinking about it.

Jesus gave to His followers everything needed to complete His divine work. In John 14:16, He said that the Father gave the Comforter, which is the Spirit of God, that the Spirit might dwell in you forever. This same Spirit has been charged to teach you all things that Jesus taught and said to His followers. The body of Christ has been busy remembering only the things Jesus said and not remembering the process of implementing His teachings. Jesus said in John (KJV) 14:12,

He that believeth on me, the works that I do shall he do also; and greater works than these shall he do, because I go unto my Father.

Paul wrote to the Thessalonians telling them that he and the other saints of God gloried in them for their patience and faith in all the persecutions and tribulations which they endured. Can we not agree that persecutions and tribulations are nothing more than the manifestation of life's problems like the ones worry attaches itself to? According to Genesis 4, they crouch at your door waiting for you to master them. Remember they desire you, and still God said that you must master them. The witnessing body at Thessalonica displayed godly characteristics that helped them to master the problems

51

of life. With whatever problems they were confronted, I believe that they pushed away worry, anxiety, fear, and yes, even depression. Paul said that their *"faith groweth exceedingly;"* they, without a doubt, were meeting the challenges of life.

The Thessalonians were displaying faith and charity, two godly characteristics that helped them to endure all of their problems. Well, if it helped the Thessalonians, then it should help you and me today. The problem is, for the most part, we do not know what faith or charity is, and we do not know how to operate within these unseen spiritual laws of faith and charity. I know that is a strong statement to make, and I also know that it is a true statement. We know more about how to worry and how to fear than how to have a God type of faith. The fact is that the witnessing body of Christ operates in such a small amount of faith that we have just enough faith to get saved and go to heaven. Apart from that, very few "mountains" are being moved throughout the whole of Christianity. We bring people to Christ in large numbers all across the world, but after they come into the family of God, what about their fruit? What about our ability to do the works that Jesus did? What about our ability to walk on water?

Faith is one of the keys to being transformed. Glory 2 God! In fact, faith is one of the most important characteristics within the movement of Jesus. Let us take a look at this unseen spiritual law called faith by asking the most obvious question, "What is faith, and how does it work?" The first thing which comes to mind for most believers is Hebrew 11:1 (KJV):

Now faith is the substance of things hoped for, the evidence of things not seen.

If we understood the full meaning of this passage, we would not have to go any further. However, the truth of the matter is that faith is still unclear to most of us. To establish this point let me ask you, "What is the substance and what is the evidence?" Think about those two questions. I would say right now that you do not have an answer, and if you think you have an answer you are probably like most of the others that I have asked this question. Let me take you on another journey in which I can explain further my teachings on the subject of faith.

I remember many years ago when I wondered about the meaning of faith. I had heard that I should let my faith loose, stretch out my faith, so that my faith could change or move mountains; and yet no one had taught me even the simple meaning of the word faith. As a result, I felt that I did not have any faith because nothing seemed to work for me. Apart from the fact that I was a member of the family of God, living by His grace, none of my prayers were being answered. No one told me what I needed to know about operating in faith; they only told me that I had to have faith.

EMUNAH: HEBREW FOR FAITH
CHAPTER 9

I did not begin to learn the meaning of faith until I was in my university undergraduate studies. It was then that I began doing word studies, and "faith" was one of the first words that I researched. Because I was studying the Old Testament and the text in the Hebrew language, I looked up this English word "faith" in the Hebrew. Faith in Hebrew is the word אמנה *emu-NAH*, and so I looked up *emunah* in the *Brown-Driver-Briggs Hebrew-English Lexicon* (BDB).

I learned that *emunah* is defined as: *firmness, steadfastness, certain, sure and sureness, established, reliable, trust and obedience.* Well, that only gave me the meaning of the word; still, since I was just starting to learn about the things of God, He had to make it very simple for me to understand. I thought, "Now how do I apply this meaning to my life? Where can I see this Hebrew meaning of faith in action?" One of the first illustrations of faith in the Bible is in Exodus 17:12, the event where the Israelites were fighting against the Amalekites. When Moses' hands became heavy and fell to his sides, the Amalekites prevailed. Aaron and Hurr held up Moses' hands and the text said that Moses' hands became *steady*, thereby the Israelites prevailed in battle. Well, there was my example of faith being used in the Scriptures. In the Old Testament the English word faith is only used a few times whereas in the New Testament, it appears over and over.

So, whatever faith is, in this text, it has something to do with being steady.

However, just because I saw the meaning of this word in the Scriptures, it did not translate into action in my life. At this time I think I had a Ph.D. in worrying, and I wanted one thing very badly and that was to learn how to stop worrying. When I took a closer look at Exodus 17:12, I saw that Israel was in a fierce battle, and I could identify with that condition. There were lots of fierce battles going on in my life at that time. As the light came on in my heart, I understood that, whatever this word faith was, I had to learn to be steady in my battles. At that time being steady was not one of the characteristics of my walk with God, still I saw that somehow I had to be steady in the battles of my life.

However, you must understand that in those early days of learning and growing in God's word, I did not learn so easily. So I cried out to God saying, "Please make it simple for me to understand!" After praying I felt the leading in my heart to look at 2 Chronicles 19:9, where the word faith was being used in the Hebrew Scriptures.

In this passage the word faith is used in connection with a perfect heart. King Jehoshapat was charged with choosing judges to sit throughout the cities. He told them that they judge not for man, but for the Lord God. It is important to note that in verse 7, the text says that with God there is no respect of persons. What I saw in those verses was that God could use me too, and that is the same for you now. His word will work in your life when applied correctly. One of the conditions by which God chooses to work His will is based upon our faith, or our steadfastness, with a perfect heart. Now a perfect heart in this case has more to do with your willingness to accept

God's way of doing things. It does not imply that you have to be one hundred percent perfect in all your action—none of us has attained that goal. We set our heart, mind, spirit to do what we have learned, and what is required of us. One of the Church's greatest mistakes is to take these words, like perfect, and try to apply them to our live without understanding how God wanted the word to be understood.

The Hebrew word for "perfect" comes from the word שָׁלוֹם (sha-LOM), and in BDB, it is defined as "completeness, wholeness, soundness." When the text tells us to act on our faith out of a perfect heart, it is saying to you where God's truths have become complete or whole in your heart, it is important that you learn to act from that part of your heart. Because it is the area where God's will is being performed, and the area where His will can be made whole in you. Let me simplify this process a little more. I know that some of you still do not understand what I am saying about acting from that area of your heart that is perfect. So let's go back to a starting point in your walk with God, i.e., when you first opened your heart and let Jesus come in. When Jesus and his Spirit came into your heart, that part of your heart where his Spirit dwells became whole, complete, perfect. When we are confronted with the conditions of life, worry is there trying to entice us. God desires that we turn our attention to that part of our heart where his Spirit dwells. Why? Because that is where our spiritual help and power await us. When you are fighting with worry or any other unseen spiritual force and it is stronger than you, always go back to your salvation experience with Jesus, and refresh your heart with the sureness of what took place when Jesus came into your heart.

YOU ARE FREE TO WORRY NO MORE

Learn To Speak It Out
Chapter 10

Before I continue with faith, let me build a foundation from which you can always have success in stopping worry in your life. In Matthew chapter four, we have the story of Jesus being tempted by the evil one. You might want to take a moment to re-read the story again. Jesus had fasted in the wilderness for forty days and forty nights. Think about Jesus not eating for that many days. You know, when you do not eat for several hours your belly begins to sing you its songs. The same conditions must have been confronting Jesus, and that element of evil Jesus called Satan came to Him saying: (author's paraphrase) "Jesus, I know you are hungry—you have not eaten in forty days. I can hear your belly growling all the way over here. Now if you are the Son of God turn these stones to bread!" The text records that Jesus said to the Tempter, *"It is written, 'Man does not live on bread alone, but on every word that comes from the mouth of God"* (Matthew 4:4, NIV). In the story the Ugly One tries again and again; still, Jesus quotes the words, "It is written" and the Scriptures tell us that he left Jesus alone.

What is important about this story is that the Evil One came to Jesus the same way he comes to you. When I took a closer look at the passages in chapter four, I could not find any words telling the reader that the Tempter came to Jesus in the natural flesh. Therefore,

I believe that the Ugly One did not appear to Jesus in a physical form. He came to Jesus the same way he comes to you and me—he spoke to His mind. Just a moment now, there is something very important about this setting. Jesus is in the wilderness all alone being tempted in a spiritual way. The way Jesus dealt with the Evil One was to speak the written word of God. I believe He spoke the word aloud! That is correct, Jesus was there alone speaking words written in the Hebrew Scriptures as if He were speaking to someone standing there. One of the first lessons I learned many years ago was to speak to the worry, fear, or any other spiritual force I was facing, and I had to speak my words out loud! You know, God showed me that when worry, fear, persecutions, tribulations—spiritual forces that crouch at our door— and try to enter our mind, we need to do the same thing Jesus did. We need to learn how to speak aloud to any element of evil coming at us, saying, "I don't receive this thought! I cast it form my mind in Jesus' name!" So that is exactly what I did. It did not matter where I was—when I felt the attack of evil coming on my mind, I started to speak aloud, casting it from me as Jesus did. I would say, "I don't receive this thought." If I had to speak those words a hundred times I was going to do so until that element of evil left me alone. Back then I did not know anything about Scriptures like, James 4:7 (KJV),

> *Submit yourselves therefore to God. Resist the devil, and he will flee from you.*

Glory! Glory 2 God! Let me return to establishing the

operation of faith in a kingdom way, so that when you take your stand against worry or any spiritual element, you will succeed!

Well, a picture was beginning to come into focus in my mind, spirit, and heart. I can look back now and see the process of transformation that was taking place within me. The only pictures I held in my mind before that time were the ones evil was showing me, and they controlled my emotions. Now a picture of what faith is and how to implement faith in my life was growing within me. I knew the meaning of faith was *firmness, steadfastness, certainty, trust* and *obedience*. I also knew that in the battles I was going through, somehow I had to display firmness in how I responded. I also knew that God expected me to implement faith from a complete heart, or from that part of my heart that He now controlled. I went on to read the next chapter and found King Jehoshaphat before the people of Israel, telling God that the people of Ammon and Moab were about to invade and take the land given to their forefathers. Jehoshaphat knew that they could not withstand the force of these people, and that the invaders would take their land unless God intervened. I could identify with this condition, and I'm sure you can as well. For me, worry was in complete control and if God did not intervene...well, you understand.

God's People Lived By Faith
Chapter 11

In 2 Chronicles 20 verse 17 (KJV), God tells Jehoshaphat that they will not have to fight in this battle. The text says that they were to

> ...set yourselves, stand ye still, and see the salvation of the Lord with you.

The picture I began to see was of a people who were given the charge to be firm, to be steadfast, to be certain, a people who were to trust and obey the Lord. The morning of the battle (verse 20), says

> ...Jehoshaphat stood and said, Hear me, O Judah, and ye inhabitants of Jerusalem; Believe in the Lord your God, so shall ye be established; believe his prophets, so shall ye prosper.

The picture was starting to clear up for me, and I pray it is doing the same for you now. In the Hebrew text, the word for "believe" is the same word as our Hebrew word *emunah* (faith) that we discussed earlier. I started to substitute English words defining *emunah* in place of "believe." What I saw set my heart on fire! I now read that Jehoshaphat said to the people of Jerusalem to be *firm, steadfast, certain, to trust and obey* the Lord their God. That seemed to be something that I could do, and yet until that moment, my actions in God were very weak. My actions followed after the elements of worry more than after God. I want to make two other points on this passage. This same Hebrew word *emunah* occurs here in the second person plural תאמנו *te-a-ME-nu* where it is translated as the English word "established." The second point deals with the word "prosper." In Hebrew it is צלח *tsah-LAKH* and can be translated as "to advance" or "to bring to successful issue."

I needed to know how to have success in God, and here in this example of faith, I found out that my ability to be firm, my ability to be steadfast, my ability to be certain, my ability to trust and obey God, not only constituted faith—it also constituted having success.

I pray that something is happening in your heart, for I remember how the process of change took hold of me. The light of kingdom began to come on in my heart, and I started to see what God expected of me. I did not understand anything about the unseen laws of God, nor did I understand how they affected my life. Paul seemed to be telling the witnessing body at Thessalonica that they were growing, and the evidence of that growth was their patience and faith. I believe most of us have difficulty in thinking of our persecutions and tribulations as being tools of God, even though Paul said they are manifest tokens of the righteous judgment of God.

Yet, in the eighteenth chapter of 2 Chronicles, the Lord asked in verse 19, 22 (KJV),

> *Who shall entice Ahab king of Israel, that he may go up and fall at Ramoth-gilead?...the Lord hath*

*put a lying spirit in the mouth of these thy prophets,
and the Lord spoke evil against thee.*

Can we not say that God's sending of this lying spirit *"is
a manifest token of the righteous judgment of God".* (1
Thessalonians 1:5, KJV)?

Oh, I firmly believe the emphasis is not on the evil
or the work of evil, but on how we react to the opportunity when evil presents its strong head. For the witnessing body at Thessalonica was developing their patience
and faith through the enduring of evil or persecution
and tribulation. I truly needed to know that, because I
had lots of persecution and tribulation like worry taking place in my life and, unlike the church at
Thessalonica, I was not enduring the trials well. I was
trying to stretch out my faith, but getting nothing in
return except more failure. When I started to learn these
simple truths, I began to implement them, and, glory!
transformation began to take place!

Still I cried out to God for more, as this word study
took shape in my life, and opened my heart to a better
understanding of faith. First, in Exodus 17:12, I learned
that whatever faith is, it has something to do with being
"steady." Then I saw faith in 2 Chronicles 20:20, a situation in which the people were unable to defeat the gi-
ant of evil they were facing. They stood fast in God,
wavering not in their trust that God could and would
do as He had said. In verse 15 (KJV) God said,

*Hearken ye, all Judah, and ye inhabitants of Jerusa-
lem, and thou king Jehoshaphat, Thus saith the Lord
unto you, Be not afraid nor dismayed by reason of*

this great multitude; for the battle is not yours, but God's.

I truly needed to know that God was there to fight my battles, because I had failed over and over at trying to get free from worry. When I think back, I can see that condition of my heart was expressed in Matthew 5:6 (KJV) which says:

> *Blessed are those who hunger and thirst for righteousness: for they shall he filled.*

As we have learned, Jesus told those who followed Him they were blessed or happy, and because they hungered and thirsted, they would be filled. I did not understand that simple truth at the time. I was crying out to God, and yet those words were a perfect picture of my life then. Yes, I was hungering and thirsting to know God—even more so to understand how to have faith. God began to lead me to the story of the three Hebrew men in Daniel chapter three. Because I was doing a word study, I looked first for the word *emunah* (faith). To my surprise, the word was not in the story at all. I then read the chapter again, and this time I noticed the key was in the situation portrayed in the story.

Nebuchadnezzar had built an image of gold and issued a decree that at the sound of the cornet, flute, harp, psaltery, dulcimer and all kinds of music, everyone that heard must fall down and worship the golden image. Whoever did not do so would be burned alive in a fiery furnace. Then the King learned there were three Jews in the land who would not fall down and worship.

The three Hebrew men (their assigned Babylonian names were Shadrach, Meshach, and Abednego) refused to fall down and worship the golden image which the king had built. They did so even in the face of knowing they would be cast into the burning fiery furnace. The king had them brought to him, and he gave them another chance, asking them, "Who is your God and will he deliver you out of my hands?" In Daniel 3:17, 18 (KJV) they replied,

> *If it be so, our God whom we serve is able to deliver us from the burning fiery furnace, and he will deliver us out of thine hand, O King. But if not, be it known unto thee, O King, that we will not serve thy gods, nor worship the golden image which thou hast set up.*

Wow-double-Wow!!! I saw faith in its purest form, not like faith as some type of logical thought that I think. Faith for the three Hebrew men was an action in which they did something. I saw a lifestyle in which you are planted in your trust and obedience of God, never moving to the conditions of life like worry. Think about this—these Hebrew men lived some eight hundred years after Moses delivered the Torah. They were taking a firm, steady, certain, action in God by trusting and obeying His word. Exodus 20:4-5 (KJV) says,

> *Thou shalt not make unto thee any graven image, or any likeness of any thing that is in heaven above, or that is in the earth beneath, or that is in the wa-*

ter under the earth. Thou shalt not bow down thyself to them, nor serve them.

I saw three Hebrew men displaying a pure type of faith *(emunah)* and they, like you and me, only had the written word. They were so willing to obey the word by being steady, firm, certain in His words, that they were willing to die in the flames before giving up the promises of God's word. 0 God in Heaven, that was what I needed to know; that was what I needed to display in my life, and Glory 2 God, I could see that this was something that even I was able to do. For the first time I began to see how I could take the word of God and be *steady*, be *firm*, be *certain*; how I could *trust and obey* God and not be moved. And yes, when it is necessary in my life, as with you, be willing to go into the fiery furnace. This, my beloved brothers and sisters in the Lord, is faith, or might I say, one portion of the concept of faith. Still, your ability to be *steadfast*, your ability to be *firm*, your ability to be certain, your ability to *trust and obey* God is an action or power which you have within you to do now! You can decide in your heart that when it comes to implementing promises of God in your life, you will display faith and not be moved. Look, the fiery furnaces of your life are nothing more than the problems you are confronted with each and every day. Those same problems are akin to persecution and tribulation that crouch at your door each and every day. Paul told the Church at Thessalonica that their faith was helping them endure things like worry, fear and depression brought on by persecutions and tribulations.

I saw clearly just what I needed to do, and at that time the sad truth was that I was not being firm, steady, trusting or obeying God. When I took my stand on a promise, the Ugly One came immediately and spoke to my mind telling me his lies. As I took the seed of the Ugly One's word I made the promise of God's word ineffective in my life. Can you see how the final actions that I took were totally opposite of the true characteristic of faith? When I looked at the Hebrew men, and how they would not doubt or be moved from God's words, I too began to know that somehow it was going to take that same kind of firmness and steadfastness in my life. It is going to take that same kind of *emunah* in yours. At first I was not ready to act as they did. When I looked at the fiery furnaces that were and might be confronting me—well, I felt the fear, and I did the same thing the children of Israel did in Exodus, the 19th chapter, verse 8 (KJV):.

Moses came down the mountain and told the people that their God wanted to make a kingdom of priests of them all. The text says that

> ...all the people answered together, and said, 'All that the Lord hath spoken we will do.'

But when they were confronted with a type of fiery furnace as in the appearance of God, the text says that they stood afar off from the mountain where God had descended. Can you imagine! God gave them the opportunity to be a nation of priests all the way back there in Exodus. Because of their fear they told Moses to go

69

alone, in their place, and be the priest, for they were afraid. The text says in verse 18,

> ...and Mount Sinai was altogether on a smoke, because the Lord descended upon it in fire: and the smoke thereof ascended as the smoke of a furnace, and the whole mountain quaked greatly.

When I looked at the story of the three Hebrew men facing their tribulation, I saw the possibility of tribulation waiting to consume me, but unlike them I gave in to the fear, the worry. At first I did not decide to enter those furnaces facing me. It was the word of God that told me that there was no fear for those who are in Christ Jesus. I knew that, and I also knew that somehow I had to travel that road if ever I was going to display faith. So with fear gripping my heart, I said to those fiery furnaces and possible furnaces, "I am going to stand firm in God and enter any and all furnaces that come my way." Yes, I had decided to face the problems, the persecutions, the tribulations that might fall upon my life, and I was going to be so *firm*, so *steadfast*, so *certain*, that I was going to trust and obey God even if the conditions would kill me.

Something powerful had started to change in my life. Prayers that went unanswered before were now being answered. With this new understanding of faith, I began to move past those problems of life that held me back. I was learning how to replace worry in my mind, heart, and spirit with a godly type of faith. You see, just like the three Hebrew men who entered the furnace and met Jesus there delivering them, I was now meeting Jesus in a more powerful manner. He was there delivering me from the worry and fear which had gripped my life for years. How great and wonderful is our God! I know that God is waiting to do the same thing in your life. Yes, right now!!

Well, I continued to study this concept called faith, for I knew that there was still more to learn. Do you remember me asking you what faith means? I ask this question in many of the meetings when I teach, and the answer given to me is usually Hebrews 11:1 (KJV):

> *Now faith is the substance of things hoped for, the evidence of things not seen.*

After hearing their response I say, "Yes, now tell me what is the substance and what is the evidence?" In my study, I came to this point of asking myself the same question. I now knew the Hebrew word for "faith" was *emunah*, and I now had the definition of the word from a reliable source. Therefore, to help you better understand Hebrews 11:1, I want you to substitute the Hebrew word *emunah* for the English word "faith." Then replace *emunah* with its English definition and as you do so you will be greatly pleased. You can make the verse personal and read it as,

> *Now my ability to be firm, my ability to be steadfast, my ability to be certain, my ability to trust and obey God is the substance of things hoped for, my ability to be firm, my ability to be steadfast, my ability to he certain, my ability to trust and obey God is the evidence of things not seen.*

Glory, Glory, Glory! My heart rushes even now as I write these words for I know that the truth of this concept is bursting alive within you right now. What a wonderful thing to know that the evidence of things you hope for will be manifest based upon your ability to be firm, steadfast, certain, trusting and obeying God. This was something I could do, and I know that it is within your ability to implement as well in your own life.

LEARNING TO DISPLAY FAITH
CHAPTER 12

Let me give you a practical example of faith in action. During the summer of 1985 my family and I were about to move to Tulsa, Oklahoma for me to enroll at Oral Roberts University. We needed a home to lease, and we drove to Tulsa to find one. I remembered coming through Tulsa a year earlier to visit the campus. While driving away, I passed a residential area about two miles north of the university on Lewis Avenue, and as I drove past the area I said a silent prayer asking God for a home in that area, pointing to the right side of the road. After we got to Tulsa, we found a home-leasing agent to help us. I remember her asking me where would I want to live. "Off South Lewis just two miles north of the campus," I said. She asked how much was I willing to pay to lease a home. Based upon what I told her, she informed me that the available homes in that area leased for about three hundred dollars more than I could pay.

Realizing that I would not be able to afford a home in that area, I began looking elsewhere. We finally settled for a home fifteen miles away from the campus. I left a security deposit with a promise to pay the first two months lease at the time of move in. We went back to Peoria and began the final stages of moving, which was about five weeks away. We left the final arrangements of having lights and gas turned on to Jackie, a close childhood friend of my wife.

About three weeks before we were to move, I received a call from Jackie, telling me that in order to turn the lights and gas on, I would have to send over five hundred dollars for the deposits. Well, I could not afford to pay the deposits and two months rent in advance at my arrival. Things were beginning to come unglued, and yes, I say worry was trying to influence me at this point. We made the adjustment by telling Jackie to find a duplex that we could lease. Within a few days she had found a place, and we felt comfortable with the arrangements. A six-month lease would give us time to search for a home for our family after moving to Tulsa. We thought that the arrangements were final until I got a call from Jackie Friday morning just five days before the move was to take place. Jackie told me that the duplex had been sold the day before, and the new owner did not want to lease. In the midst of what should have been panic and lots of anxiety, worry, fear, and even some depression, this is what I did. Worry was telling me that I needed to leave right away and drive to Tulsa to find a home; after all, it took almost a week to find the first home when we were there.

The reality, however, was that it was our last weekend in the city, and two churches had asked me to speak, one on Sunday morning and the other Sunday night. I remember thinking about how I had given my word to be there. After all, it was our last Sunday in Peoria, and there were dear friends counting on seeing my family and me for the last time. Still, there was this voice inside telling me that they would understand why I would have to break my word. There was this voice painting pictures in my mind of the troubles awaiting me in finding a home, pressuring me to leave right away.

That Friday morning after hearing from Jackie concerning the sale of the duplex, deep down inside me I knew what I had to do. I told my wife that I was not leaving until I had fulfilled our promises. I knew that God wanted the move from Peoria to Tulsa, and I knew that He had a home there for my family. Well, I spoke in both churches that Sunday morning and night, then drove all night and arrived in Tulsa about 8:00 am that Monday morning. I found another leasing agent near the University, and the lady asked me in what area would we like to live. I told her about the area two miles north of the campus, and she said, "we just got a new listing this morning for a home just off Lewis and 56th street." Before noon that day I had signed a lease on a home in a neighborhood where the homes leased for hundreds more than I could afford. The owner of the home learned why I was moving to Tulsa, and he lowered the payments to accommodate my family's needs.

God is wonderful, and all He asks of us is to implement His words in our lives. Faith is to determine in our hearts that we will no longer waver back and forth on the promises of God. I have been on a long journey seeking to have and to understand faith, and I took my family from city to city, from meeting to meeting seeking to find God's teachings on faith. Back then I believed that faith was some kind of supernatural element that God zaps you with, causing you to suddenly walk in power and authority. I was praying to God for more faith, and all the time faith was waiting for me to learn how to be *firm, steady, certain,* how to *trust and obey God.* As I think back to those days when worry was controlling my life such as when one of my children was away from home and I did not know what to do, it is clear now how faith was the answer to my needs then as it is today. And all I needed to do was to decide to be *firm, steadfast, certain,* to *trust and obey* God even when I did not know what the outcome was going to be. Years later, when I began to understand faith from the Hebraic perspective, I was able to look back and find experiences where faith operated, where my actions were consistent with the true meaning of the word. I pray now that you are using this teaching to look at your life and to see how you, too, can become more consistent in your walk with God.

I am not able to find the words to express how I felt when I began to understand what was expected of me concerning my walk in faith. I used to think that faith was for those great men and women of God in the Bible, and a few that walk in faith today. All the while faith was a simple principle that even I, and surely you, can walk in each day. I challenge you to start right now. Yes, start now to implement being *firm, steadfast, certain, trusting and obeying* God's promises. When life brings its problems and sets them at the door of your being, you have to refuse the thought of worry, and choose the promises of God.

When I made this choice, I discovered that for the first time life was not ruling me. I was having victory over conditions that had ruled and controlled me for years. I was facing my fiery furnaces. That is right, I was entering the fiery furnace of worry, of anxiety, of fear, of depression—all those things that gripped my heart and stopped me from walking uprightly before the Lord. This concept of faith was coming alive in my heart, and

I am believing that it is doing the same for you. As my understanding grew, I felt the Spirit of God teaching me, as Jesus said the Spirit would do in John the 14th chapter. I want you to know that you should let the Holy Spirit in you teach you the promises of God. You should especially call upon the Spirit to help you make faith become your natural response in your walk with God. Jesus said one of the special functions of the Spirit is to bring or, might I say, to cause the things of Jesus/God to be remembered in us. I need all the help I can get. Thank You God, for sending Your Spirit to teach us and to help us to know Your way in a difficult world.

YOU ARE FREE TO WORRY NO MORE

A Second Level Of Faith

Chapter 13

While at Oral Roberts University, in a class with my dear friend Dr. Brad Young, I wrote a term paper and the subject was—yes, "faith." It was during my work on that research paper that the Spirit showed me there are two levels of faith. I remember discussing the paper with Dr. Young in his office. He asked me, "Where did you get that there were two levels of faith?" I answered him. He then asked, when did you first see that there are two levels of faith? I gave him my answer, and he confirmed that I was correct in this statement. When I left his office I remembered thinking about his questions, how he asked where did I get this concept. I made this statement in my paper that there were two levels of faith, and because it was an academic paper, a citation of credit must be given when using the words of another author.

However, there was no other author to give credit to because it was the Comforter/Holy Spirit revealing this simple principle to my heart. What a wonderful feeling, a mentor was confirming that what the Spirit of God had revealed in my heart was true. Dr. Young's second question was, "When did you first see that there are two levels of faith?" His question caused me to search my heart, to bring it to my remembrance, and as I did, I felt as if Jesus, by way of His Spirit, was speaking and teaching me. I also remember thinking that Dr. Young may have thought that I had plagiarized by taking someone

YOU ARE FREE TO WORRY NO MORE

else's statement without proper credit. The fact was that the Spirit, the same Spirit that lives and dwells in you, revealed to me that there are two levels of faith.

For the believer this is very important because it takes the child of God into the most powerful realm of the Spirit there is. The supernatural, where calling those things that are not as though they are, operates God's Kingdom. Jesus said in Matthew 17:20 (KJV):

> *If ye have faith as a grain of mustard seed, ye shall say unto this mountain, remove hence to yonder place; and it shall remove; and nothing shall be impossible unto you.*

WOW! Before I explain the second level of faith, I want to speak to many of you who are already walking *firmly, steadfastly, certainly*—you who are well able to *trust and obey* God. The thing that is missing in your walk is the knowledge you need to access the divine power of God. You have read the scripture, and you know the promises are established and that every believer should be able to speak to the mountains of his or her life and see them totally removed. Still, you also know that that level of divine power just does not operate in the life of the church at large.

Your answer is found in Galatians 2:20 (KJV), where the text says:

> *I am crucified with Christ, nevertheless I live: yet not I, but Christ lives in me; and the life which I now live in the flesh I live by the faith of the Son of God who loved me, and gave himself for me.*

I should not have to go any further. The above passage really says it all. First of all, Paul is saying that he, as well as you and I, was crucified with Jesus, yet he, as well as you and I, still lives. However, and this is a powerful "however," if the process of being dead or dying with Christ were completed in us, neither you nor I would live. That is to say, only Christ would live in us, for the process that we access would have transformed us into who and what He is. Therefore, the life that we should be living in the flesh on this earth, we live (and please get this) we live by the faith of the Son of God. Oh my Lord, did you get that?

Too long has the witnessing body (you and I, the Church) tried to move the mountains of our lives with our own faith. The mountains are not going anywhere because God never asked you to move a mountain with your own faith. Jesus only commanded us to have faith in God (Mark 11:22). Please note that the second level of faith is the one hundred percent perfect, never failing faith of Jesus, which moves absolutely every mountain in your life. All God asks of you and me is to be *firm, steadfast, certain,* to *trust and obey* Him. Then and only then does the perfect faith of the Son of God manifest itself for you. Moving the mountains from your life is not your responsibility; it belongs to God. Your responsibility is never to doubt the promises of God, not even for a split second.

When the three Hebrew men were told that they were going to be thrown into a fiery furnace, I believe that fear must have been there gripping their hearts. I believe that worry, anxiety, and yes, even depression were right there pulling at their minds, crying out to them to choose one of them. Yet, in the face of all their tribulations they chose to display faith in their God, the type of faith that released the second level of faith, the faith of the Son of Man, the supernatural power of God, and it delivered them. What a lesson for us to learn today, because we too face the pressures of life, and our success in being a reflection of Jesus in this world depends on our ability to be firm, to be steadfast, to be certain, to trust and obey God. I tell you, just as Jesus was there in the furnace delivering the Hebrew men, He is here now, ready, waiting for you to display that same type of firmness, certainty, steadfastness in God, which will release His divine power, or might I say, the second level of faith, for you in your life.

Now I know many of you are questioning whether there is such a thing as a second level of faith. Therefore let us establish this point with the evidence of the Word of God. Let me point out that God is not calling you to move mountains, or might I be more personal, God is not commanding you to move the problems of persecution or tribulation out of your life with your own faith. What God is commanding you to do is simply to be firm in Him. In Matthew 8:5-8 (KJV), the text says:

> *When Jesus was entered into Capernaum, there came unto him a centurion, beseeching him, and saying, Lord, my servant lieth at home sick of the palsy, grievously tormented. And Jesus saith unto him, I will come and heal him.. The centurion answered and said, Lord, I am not worthy that thou shouldest come under my roof but speak the word*

only, and my servant shall be healed. For I am a man under authority, having soldiers under me: and I say to this man, Go, and he goeth; and to another, Come, and he cometh!; and to my servant, Do this, and he doeth it. When Jesus heard it, he marveled, and said to them that followed, Verily I say unto you, I have not found so great faith, no, not in Israel.

First of all, the centurion knew what it meant to have authority. When I read these passages in the Hebrew text, the simple actions of the centurion are more clear than they are in the English text. The centurion used Go! Come! Do!—all of which were in the imperative, which states a command. Can you see the centurion giving a command to his soldiers, and then sitting down and worrying about whether his men were going to do what he had commanded? No, not at all. I spent two years in the Army, and one of the first things I learned was to do what I was being told by those who had the authority.

The point that I am establishing for you is that Jesus does not ask you to move a mountain or problem with your faith. Jesus said of the centurion that He had not found such great faith in all of Israel, or as the New International Version puts it; *"I have not found anyone in Israel with such great faith."* My question to you is, "If the centurion had such great faith, why did he not use his faith to heal his servant who was sick in his home?"

Jesus was acknowledging the *steadfastness*, the *firmness*, the *certainty*, the *willingness to trust and obey* the one who had all power and authority, which was Himself. The centurion is our example of how faith operates. He came to Jesus, or might I say, he plugged his ability to be *certain*, to be *steadfast*, to be *firm*, to *trust and obey*, into Jesus, and then and only then was his servant healed. He acted just like the three Hebrew men, who plugged their *emunah* (faith) into God, and Jesus met them in the midst of their problem and delivered them.

I am sure you will agree that it was by Jesus' faith that the centurion's servant was healed. The text records in verse 13 that Jesus said to the centurion, *"Go thy way!"* using the imperative as in a command which, as a soldier, he understood very well. Then Jesus said, *"...as you have believed,"* meaning that as you have placed the problem, the thing that was persecuting you and your servant, in My hand, Jesus' hands. So as you have displayed your firmness, your steadfastness, your certainty, your ability to trust and obey Jesus, *"so be it done unto thee, and his servant was healed in the same hour."*

This, my dear friends, is the second level of faith. It is the one hundred-percent perfect faith of the Son of Man who gave himself for you that you might be changed into what God intended from the beginning. Yes, this is the supernatural, the kingdom which Jesus said will manifest on your behalf when you display the simple principle of having faith in God. Oh, glory 2 God! You see, the day that I began to live my life each day by the faith of Jesus, was also the day that all the weight I carried on my shoulders fell by my side and I felt so free in Jesus. When you begin to live your life by the faith of Jesus, then and only then will you be able to stop this spiritual force of worry in your life.

Let's return to our primary text found in Matthew
6:25. I am going to quote the first part of this text in
Hebrew to express my last point. It reads:

עַל כֵּן אוֹמֵר אֲנִי לָכֶב אַל תִדְאֲגוּ

Our English translation of this text simply says, *"Therefore I tell you, do not worry...!"* (NIV) Hebrew is read
from right to left and thus the first word of this sentence
is עַל *al* and the last word is the subject of this book,
worry תִדְאֲגוּ *tid-a-GU* Jesus is speaking to His audience
telling them of the principles of His kingdom, a kingdom in which the supernatural has dominion over the
natural realm we live in today. What is important about
this text is its syntax. According to *Gesenius' Hebrew
Grammar* the Hebrew word תִדְאֲגוּ comes from the root
דְאַג *DA-agh* and is an imperative; thus, when Jesus used
the word תִדְאֲגוּ, He was speaking in command form. We,
as followers of Jesus, want to obey the words of God and
the words of Jesus. Because Jesus used the imperative, a
command, it is clear that we are to obey those words.
Now the simple truth of this matter is that each time
you take thought or worry, you are entering the world
of sin. Yes, that is true, when you worry you sin, and
sin is not pleasing to God. I included this information
at the end of this book to let you know how important
it is for you to learn how to stop worrying. I also believe
that you, just like me, want to please God with all your
heart, spirit, and mind. This book has unmasked the
work of worry and set a direction whereby you can implement simple principles that will absolutely work in your

life. These are the principles of Kingdom, and I know your life will never be the same.

Let me end with a prayer: *Father, thank you for your help in writing this book. Thank you for Your Spirit guiding me, and now Your Spirit is setting free those who read this book. Lord, I believe with all my heart that the same power which helped me to stop worrying is at work now in the reader's heart, doing the same for him or her. I believe this because I know it is not me, Lord—it is You. All glory and honor unto You most High God, with love!*